The Perfect Meeting

THE PERFECT SERIES

ALL YOU NEED TO GET IT RIGHT FIRST TIME

OTHER TITLES IN THE SERIES:

The Perfect Appraisal
Howard Hudson ISBN 0–7126–5541–7

The Perfect CV
Max Eggert ISBN 0–7126–5546–8

The Perfect Dismissal
John McManus ISBN 0–7126–5641–3

Perfect Financial Ratios
Terry Gasking ISBN 0–7126–5529–8

The Perfect Interview
Max Eggert ISBN 0–7126–5073–3

The Perfect Negotiation
Gavin Kennedy ISBN 0–7126–5465–8

The Perfect Presentation
Andrew Leigh and Michael Maynard
ISBN 0–7126–5536–0

The Perfect Meeting

ALL YOU NEED
TO GET IT RIGHT
FIRST TIME

DAVID SHARMAN

ARROW
BUSINESS BOOKS

Copyright © David Sharman 1993
The right of David Sharman to be identified as the author of this
work has been asserted by him in accordance with the Copyright,
Designs and Patents Act 1988

First published in Great Britain by
Century Business
An imprint of Random House UK Limited
20 Vauxhall Bridge Road, London SW1V 2SA

Random House Australia (Pty) Limited
20, Alfred Street, Milsons Point, Sydney,
New South Wales 2061, Australia

Random House New Zealand Limited
18 Poland Road, Glenfield
Auckland 10, New Zealand

Random House South Africa (Pty)
PO Box 337, Bergvlei, South Africa

10 9 8 7 6 5 4

Set in Bembo by
SX Composing Ltd., Raleigh, Essex
Printed and bound in Great Britain by
Cox & Wyman Ltd, Reading, Berkshire

British Library Cataloguing in Publication Data
A catalogue record for this book is available from the British
Library.

ISBN 0-7126-5593-X

ACKNOWLEDGEMENTS

I should like to thank Ted Johns for all the support and expertise that he has provided over many years. Meetings were always good fun when he was around!

Grateful thanks to Ros during the writing phase; and dedicated to Marina and Caroline to help them in their futures.

ABOUT THE AUTHOR

David Sharman is an independent management consultant, specializing in creativity, management, team-
work and organizational development programmes.
He is a Fellow of the Institute of Personnel Management, and for many years worked as a Senior Lecturer
at the Thames Valley University, teaching in the
Management Centre. During this period he attended
many meetings, and learned a great deal about how to
look alert without really trying.

Before that he worked as either a personnel or training officer in both the private and public sector. This
book condenses many years of experience; some negative, others highly creative. Currently he is using and
researching the 'learning community' model of meetings as convenor of the Association of Management
Education and Development Green Network. Getting
even more flexibility and participation into meetings –
without losing any creativity, is still a primary concern.

To exchange you own 'war stories' of meetings you
have attended, or any new flexible and participative
processes, please contact him at:

55, Mayhill Road, London, SE7 7JG.
Tel: 081–305–2196

CONTENTS

Introduction   viii

1. **Why Meetings Fail**   1

2. **Planning for the Meeting**   8

3. **Before the Meeting**   14

4. **The Meeting in Process**   20

5. **The Skills of the Chairperson**   29

6. **Improving Participation**   39

7. **Participation, Presentation and Influencing Skills**   47

8. **Review and Follow up**   60

Appendix A   Rules of Order   65

Appendix B   Minutes of Meetings   67

Appendix C   How to Wreck Meetings   69

Appendix D   Meetings Review: A Group Training Exercise   72

Appendix E   Review of Participation at Meetings   74

References   76

INTRODUCTION

We can't go on meeting like this!
(Audit Commission Report)

The whole question of the number and length of meetings, and their purpose, was thrown up by this report, which cited two local education authorities. One had a budget of £230 million and held 32 meetings a year on education, while the other with a budget of £160 million held 302.

We can see from the above that it is the *quality* of meetings that counts not the *quantity*.

This book is written for anyone who has to participate in meetings. I firmly believe that *anyone* present has the power to take action to improve the conduct of a meeting – whether in a work setting or as part of leisure or social life. *The Perfect Meeting* tells you where to start that improvement, and how to go about it.

For the purpose of this book 'a meeting' can be defined as a business or professionally orientated gathering of two or more people. There are literally as many kinds of meeting as there are kinds of people who attend them. I believe that the same basic rules of good management can be applied to every meeting – whether it is a sales, staff, negotiation, board or other type of meeting, the fundamental principles are the same. The same rules apply to the organizer, chairperson or straightforward participant; it is merely their roles that are different.

Chapter 1 outlines reasons why meetings may fail to achieve their purpose and suggests some solutions. The next chapters (2, 3 and 4) give some detailed guidance on a positive approach to organizing and then conducting a routine meeting. Bearing in mind the significant role of the chairperson I have devoted an entire chapter (5) to looking at the chairperson's role in some detail.

Chapter 6 provides some guidance on how to improve participation at meetings, using a range of practical examples that you can apply to your own situation.

The term 'chairperson' is used throughout the book to describe the person primarily responsible for initiating, structuring and then running a meeting. The only exception occurs in Chapter 6 on 'Improving Participation', where the word facilitator is used deliberately to emphasize that a different style is required in order to ensure increased participation from the meeting. Clearly the chairperson may take on the role of facilitator on many occasions – just as the facilitator may have to exert his or her authority as chairperson from time to time.

Chapter 7 deals specifically with the role of the individual participant, outlining ways everyone can present themselves more positively at meetings. In addition, issues surrounding the 'hidden agenda' and lobbying are considered in the context of using specific tactics to influence the course of a meeting.

To conclude, I have looked at one of the most important parts of the meeting process – the follow-up action to be taken. This must be clear and unambiguous, so that it generates commitment from everyone who has attended.

Chapter 8 offers guidelines on assessing the meetings you currently organize or attend. It describes the idea of the 'meeting audit' – a way of measuring the relative success of meetings.

This book contains some material on procedures and routines, but seeks mainly to emphasize the crucial aspect of process, or *how* a meeting is conducted, rather than *what* is discussed.

Lastly I invite all readers to consider whether they agree that 90 per cent of the perfect meeting happens before it takes place!

WHY MEETINGS FAIL

No organization can really function without meetings. After all, how else does one department communicate with another? How, indeed, do colleagues discuss shared problems and their possible solutions? Whether a regular, formal event or a more ad hoc arrangement, meetings should always be an integral part of working life.

With the global trend away from an industrial economy (with fewer decision makers and more 'doers') towards an information/service-based economy (where localized decision making is a daily necessity) meetings now provide a more significant area of employee participation than ever before. A recent study predicted a further five to nine per cent increase in the frequency of meetings over the next five years.

This book will show how any meeting can be run in such a way that it enriches the working lives of its participants, generating co-operation and commitment to higher levels of performance.

To understand the importance of meetings, and why they can fail, it is first necessary to consider the many functions they serve.

FUNCTIONS OF THE MEETING

Rapid decision making
Almost all views of the future indicate the need to cope with ever-increasing rates of change. Decision making must therefore become more efficient to catch up. Effective meetings are a valuable means of bringing together key people to discuss, then resolve, issues that could affect large numbers of staff.

Disseminating information

Through meetings, a good deal of information can be effectively passed on – information which might otherwise be unclear or uninteresting (and therefore unheeded) in written 'memo' form. The format of the meeting encourages two-way communication. The more involved the staff feel in the process, the more likely they are to take ownership of the information and ideas presented to them.

Internal changes

A great deal of resistance to change stems from staff feeling that they are not being consulted over issues, or long-term plans, that directly concern them. Any organization that intends to follow a new direction or adopt new policies will need to bring staff together as often as possible.

Through consultation on new policies and procedures, meetings can be a means for working through the need for change and the methods of implementation. The end result will be considerably more successful than leaving staff 'in the dark', uninvolved and resentful.

External changes

For an increasing number of organizations, change in their external business environment is now so rapid that the corresponding need to share information internally is vital. This could be information about their competitors, the general economic climate, press coverage of their products and so forth.

After all, sales personnel are often better placed than senior management to gauge the changing needs of the market, via their day-to-day contact with actual customers. Meetings provide a situation where such knowledge can be passed on to key decision-makers or other departments.

Regular meetings can also draw together significant pieces of information from different departments, allowing all those affected by changes or decisions to be presented with a 'total picture'. Again, this will foster a willing commitment and increased co-operation arising from any decisions made at the meeting.

Exchange of ideas and experience

While memos are merely able to circulate information, meetings can both encourage comment on that information and aid further development of the ideas put forward. By bringing together a number of different perspectives, meetings can produce new ideas or new ways of solving problems that may not have been considered before.

Many interesting creative methods can be employed in a group situation to develop new approaches to long-standing problems. A useful and stimulating technique is 'brainstorming'. This generates a large number of ideas from a group of people in a short space of time, by encouraging them to contribute ideas in a spontaneous, unselfconscious way.

Developing teamwork

When members of staff need to work closely together, meetings can be a means of dissipating suspicion and fear of the unknown. They can also help to overcome unhealthy rivalry.

The same is true when there have been recent changes or upheavals that have not been fully explained to staff. To gain a favourable outcome the meeting should help to develop mutual respect and understanding amongst the participants by involving them in a co-operative process.

WHY MEETINGS FAIL

The meeting was unnecessary!

The real purpose of the meeting had probably not been adequately thought through by the organizer. As a result, the participants may have become frustrated or dissatisfied, feeling that their time and effort had been wasted on something that could have been dealt with more effectively in some other way.

Solution – Consider in what other ways information could be distributed (by telephone, letter or fax, for instance).

The purpose of the meeting was not clear

The aim in the mind of the organizer was not really shared by – or adequately communicated to – the participants. No adjustment to their differing points of view had been made by the chairperson.

Without a shared view of the purpose of the meeting, it is difficult for the chairperson to guide those in attendance. Vagueness surrounding the actual objectives may lead participants into unhelpful areas of 'pet grievance' or other irrelevances.

Solution – Define goals before meetings and share them with participants as often and as quickly as possible.

The meeting was badly planned and ill-prepared

The meeting obviously lacked structure, bereft of an effective agenda which should have been available to participants at the start of the meeting or, ideally, well beforehand. Without adequate briefing as to the purpose of the meeting, the participants will have had no opportunity to prepare effectively.

Solution – Plan and distribute the agenda before the meeting.

The meeting was held in a poor environment

Where, and when, a meeting takes place will have a significant impact on its eventual success or failure. A meeting held in uncomfortable surroundings – oppressive heat or bitter cold – is unlikely to stimulate worthwhile contributions from those present. Similarly, overcrowding will interfere with the quality of communication, the resultant discomfort again serving to distract participants from the matter in hand.

Solution – Visit the venue before the meeting and check up on the facilities available.

The meeting was disrupted

Constant interruptions, or background noise, will disrupt the flow of the discussion – acting like static or interference on a television set.

Solution – Check likely interruptions before the meeting. Delegate urgent business and make it clear that participants are not to be disturbed.

The wrong people were present – and the right people were absent!

Having too many participants at the meeting may inhibit frank and free discussion. Too few, on the other hand, may provide an unrepresentative view of the overall problem or issues to be discussed.

Solution – Key individuals, with authority to make and implement the necessary decisions, must be identified and invited to attend. Effective decisions cannot be made by people who have no means of implementing them.

The chairperson was not adequate

The chairperson must be sure to fulfil a guiding and facilitating role – if he or she is too dogmatic, or obviously weak, the participants will reflect this by feeling either intimidated or resentful, and co-operation will suffer as a result.

Solution – The chairperson needs to develop skills in defining the structure of the discussion and guiding the processes of the meeting. He or she must remain sensitive to the needs or feelings of those attending the meeting, knowing when to draw out the reticent members and when to curb those who are prone to being overbearing.

Nothing was decided!
Allowing participants too much latitude, however, can lead to all kinds of unhelpful digressions as they vent their spleen on pet subjects. As the meeting veers further from the agenda it becomes less likely that any decisions will be taken or actions agreed.

Solution – The chairperson must carefully and firmly guide the meeting through the agenda, ensuring that there are no major departures from the subjects agreed for discussion.

THE PERFECT MEETING – PRELIMINARY CHECKLIST

- **Purpose** – All participants know and understand the purpose of the meeting and its desired outcomes
- **Agenda** – The framework upon which the meeting rests, organized to achieve the purpose and outcomes of the meeting
- **Participants** – Those with insights or expertise are invited to attend, along with those who have the authority to implement agreed action. They come prepared, understand their roles and are able to make contributions in an open, positive way
- **Chairperson** – The chairperson guides the discussion with reference to the agenda, accommodating the varying needs and sensitiveness of those present and keeping the meeting heading in the direction of the desired outcome
- **Agreed action** – Before the meeting is over the chairperson should summarize clearly what has been achieved and agreed
- **Follow-up** – The meeting secretary records all the decisions and action points in the minutes, so that everyone can easily see what they are required to contribute to the agreed action from the meeting

2

PLANNING FOR THE MEETING

This chapter views meetings from the perspective of the chairperson, as most of the burden for planning and preparation will usually fall on the chairperson's shoulders. Nevertheless, each individual participant can, and *should*, take responsibility for the successful outcome of the meeting.

Separate sections in this chapter and the next outline the planning and preparation that participants can do themselves.

TYPES OF MEETING

- **Informative/Advisory**
  - both to give and receive information and thereby to keep 'in touch'
  - to co-ordinate activities
  - to record progress towards stated goals

- **Consultative**
  - resolving objections
  - involving people in change or a new course of action
  - simply to 'get to know' people, as a means of fostering greater understanding between colleagues

- **Problem-solving**
  - to create ideas
  - to identify alternative courses of action
  - to initiate that action

- **Decision-taking**
  - to generate commitment
  - to take decisions

- to share responsibility
- to initiate action

- **Negotiating**
  - to create an agreement or contract
  - to find the best solution, quite often a mutually agreeable compromise

WHY HAVE A MEETING?

As chairperson, your first priority at the planning stage is to review the main purpose of the meeting – even question whether it is really necessary at all? Would other courses of action be more likely to yield the desired outcome?

Alternatives to meetings

- **An executive decision** – Sometimes a manager has the necessary information to take a decision without any further consultation.
- **The memo, letter, fax or electronic mail message** – If the objective is to pass on non–controversial information to other members of staff then written communication may be cheaper and more effective.
- **The telephone** – Simply engaging in a few important two–way discussions over the telephone with the key individuals concerned can render a meeting superfluous.
- **The video teleconference** – Already a viable alternative for many organizations. Long–distance telephone contact with a video link–up can greatly reduce the need for costly foreign travel.

What do you want the meeting to achieve?

Establish, then think through, what you feel could be the most effective outcome to the issue at hand. Consider whether this is attainable in one meeting, or is simply a staging post on the way to something else?

- **The ideal outcome?** – Get all the key objectives agreed, in terms that everyone can understand.

- **The realistic outcome?** – Get about half the key objectives fully discussed and agreed by everyone.
- **The fall-back position?** – Have a full and frank discussion of the objectives, identifying blocks to progress from each person.

Considering these possible outcomes can be helpful in two ways. First, it focuses *your* attention on the ultimate objectives of the meeting, on how everyone will benefit as a result. In addition, it will pinpoint the options that are available and allow you to retain a clear view of what you want to achieve.

PLANNING

Who should attend?
At this stage you should be able to assess who will need to attend and, more importantly, who will *not* need to attend. This prevents staff wasting their time attending a meeting to no apparent purpose, which is frustrating for everyone.

At regular, routine meetings attendance is rarely an issue. At other times there may be scope for bringing in outside influences, experts for instance, who can enliven the meeting by offering new perspectives or sound, well-informed advice.

It may also prove helpful to introduce 'disinterested parties' who can be seen, by all sides, to give an impartial view. Such people can act as useful catalysts in otherwise difficult negotiations.

In general terms, the following people need to be included:

- Those with information to give to the meeting
- Those who will gather useful information from the meeting

- Those with expertise to contribute to the meeting
- Those who, for the sake of office protocol, need to be invited
- Those who may be able to provide balance in areas of instability or conflict
- Those who are empowered to implement any actions agreed

Setting the agenda

This is a crucial task for the chairperson, as it defines the boundaries of the discussion that will ensue in the course of the meeting. In effect, *whoever controls the agenda, controls the meeting*.

The agenda has many functions:

- It can communicate certain expectations to everyone involved, well in advance of the meeting
- Later it will act as a script, or mechanism, via which the chairperson can steer the meeting
- Ultimately, it will also serve as a standard or measure of success

A carefully planned agenda is the most valuable tool for keeping the group mind focused on achieving the desired outcome. In effect, it is a 'map' of the meeting that everyone can refer to.

Even for short meetings of two or three people, the very act of thinking through and developing an agenda can lead to a structure that will focus on the outcomes that all those involved really want.

Creating an effective agenda

- Consider carefully who should attend
- Cover a few major points or issues which have a common thread

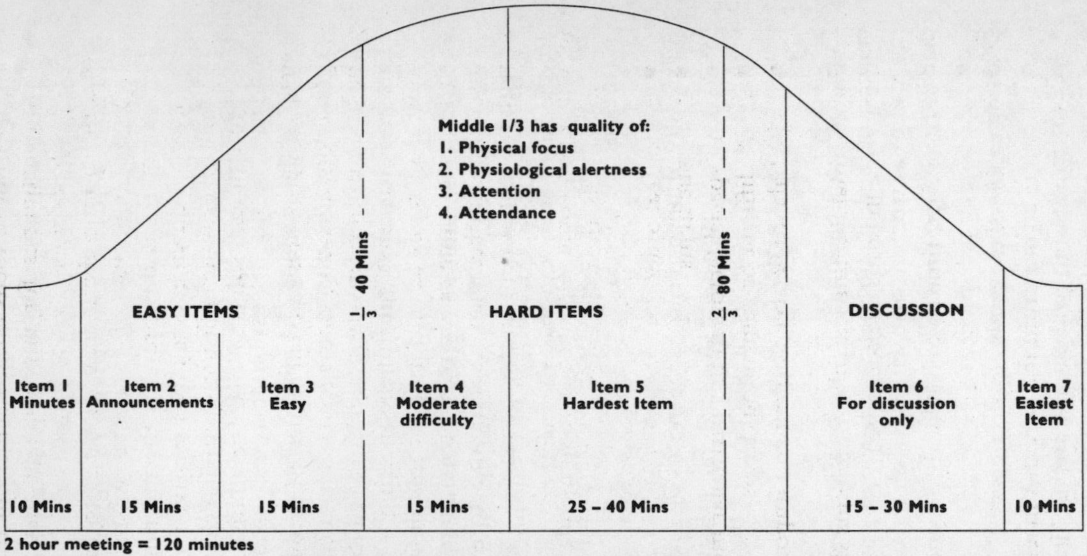
Middle 1/3 has quality of:
1. Physical focus
2. Physiological alertness
3. Attention
4. Attendance
EASY ITEMS
1/3 40 Mins
HARD ITEMS
2/3 80 Mins
DISCUSSION
Item 1 Minutes
Item 2 Announcements
Item 3 Easy
Item 4 Moderate difficulty
Item 5 Hardest Item
Item 6 For discussion only
Item 7 Easiest Item
10 Mins
15 Mins
15 Mins
15 Mins
25 – 40 Mins
15 – 30 Mins
10 Mins
2 hour meeting = 120 minutes

Figure 2.1 Structuring the agenda
Reprinted with kind permission of Sage Publications Inc
from *Effective Meetings: improving group decision-making* by J. E. Tropman, 1980.

- Structure the agenda carefully, but loosely, to allow scope for discussion
- Try not to focus on problems, but to look at the opportunities for improvement they represent – keep positive
- Be specific about time allocated to each issue or topic (e.g. use of executive washroom – five minutes), as this prevents the meeting becoming bogged down in detail over relatively minor issues and gives some indication as to the relevant import-ance of each subject in the overall discussion.

The structure illustrated in Figure 2.1 provides a useful guide to sequencing your agenda. The meeting should build up from relatively straightforward items for dis-cussion – the first third of the meeting – to reach the most challenging items during the middle stages. From there, the meeting can move to items merely requiring discussion, rather than resolution, before concluding with the easiest item on the agenda.

When you come to sequence your agenda you should also consider the following:

- A logical order
- Routine items
- Any special factors in this particular meeting
- Any difficult or contentious items
- The balance between urgent and important topics

For a formal meeting the following items should be on the agenda in terms of procedure:

- Title, date, time and place of the meeting
- Apologies for absence
- Minutes of the previous meeting
- Matters arising from the previous meeting
- Other items to be discussed and decided
- Any other business
- Date, time and place of the next meeting

3

BEFORE THE MEETING

After the date, time and location of the meeting have been decided, and the agenda set, there is still much preparation to be done. It is a common, and costly, failing that people spend too little time in preparation and too much time in meeting.

Consider the fact that 90 per cent of an effective meeting is said to happen *before* it takes place.

All too often, time is wasted within a meeting on matters that could, and should, have been resolved beforehand. Similarly, time and effort may be wasted on un-doing problems that could have been avoided altogether with a bit of forethought.

PLANNING FOR PEOPLE

As chairperson, an important part of your preparation involves thinking through the proposed meeting long before it takes place. In other words exploring all the possibilities, understanding and identifying possible sticking points and thus being able to *pre-empt* them.

By considering the probable needs, wants and motivations of the participants you will be able to estimate the likely course of the meeting and can approach it more comprehensively prepared.

Questions to help your preparation

- Who will be at the meeting?
- What are they particularly concerned about, or interested in?
- What are their aims, aspirations and assumptions about the meeting – particularly where contentious issues are likely to arise?

- How do you envisage reconciling these individual aims, aspirations and assumptions into a coherent whole?
- Who has authority to get things done?
- What are your priorities for achieving the desired outcomes – and what particular issues might get in the way of you achieving them?
- How can you ensure that *all* those participating prepare effectively for the meeting?

Pre-meeting papers and notifying people

Obviously, as chairperson, you must familiarize yourself with any meeting papers or relevant information sent out with the agenda. Less obviously, but equally important, you must encourage everyone participating in the meeting to do *their* 'homework'.

One way of doing this is to get into the habit of starting the meeting with the clear assumption that everyone *is* properly prepared. Participants will rapidly understand that valuable time will *not* be devoted to debating minor details of pre-meeting papers – or demotivating those who have prepared diligently by reiterating information for those who haven't!

Preparation checklist

So, when you come to prepare for the meeting, make sure you have allowed time for the following:

- Doing your own 'homework' on the agenda
- Notifying all participants in good time
- Making sure that all who are invited can attend
- Making sure the meeting room is ready
- Making sure participants have enough time to meet any special technical needs for the meeting – visual aids, presentations etc.

PLANNING FOR PLACE

Physical location

Do make sure that someone visits the location before the meeting to check its suitability. If there are doubts about numbers of participants you should aim for a degree of flexibility in the layout. Can unnecessary furniture or fittings be removed to create more space, for instance? If the venue *does* prove to be unsuitable you must have enough time to organize an alternative.

It is also important to run through a checklist of features or facilities that the venue has available:

- Are there enough chairs?
- Will it have any tables, audio–visual equipment or overhead projectors etc. that you may require?
- If you need to bring in your own audio–visual equipment etc. will there be enough accessible power points to cater for it?
- Who will be in charge of the booking and maintenance of such equipment?
- Because of the room's location are there likely to be distractions – trains passing close by, orchestra rehearsals etc. – at particular times of the day?
- Is there adequate heating, lighting and ventilation for the type of meeting you are holding?

Planning the room layout

Every effort should be made to ensure that the room layout is conducive to good contact between all the participants. Everyone should be able to see and hear each other clearly. The room should be large enough to hold the meeting in comfort, but small enough to maintain atmosphere – making sure that participants don't feel distanced from each other.

Comfortable chairs also have a significant role to play – particularly in a long meeting. After all, you want people to be concentrating on the matter in hand, not shifting in their seats, desperately trying to restore the circulation to their aching behinds!

Adapting the room layout

With a bit of thought, it can be relatively easy to adapt an existing layout to suit your purposes. First, you must

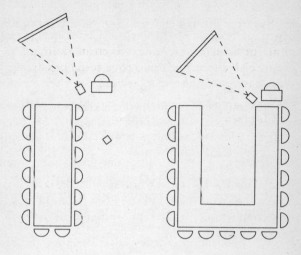

3.1   **3.2**

Figure 3.1 Conference table (suitable for under 20 people) – promotes discussion

Figure 3.2 U-shaped tables (suitable for under 30 people) – promotes discussion

Figure 3.3 Classroom style (suitable for any size)

Figure 3.4 Theatre-style (suitable for any size)

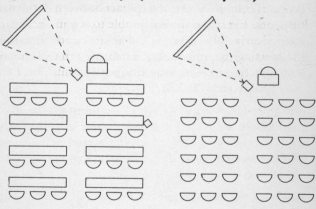

3.3   **3.4**

put fixtures, fittings and furniture into the following categories:

- **Fixed** – For instance the walls, which tend to be permanent
- **Semi-fixed** – Partitions or staging and platforms
- **Flexible** – Chairs and tables, of course, also projectors, televisions (unless wall-bracketed) and other audio–visual equipment

Special note – The most common mistake is for people to treat *semi-fixed* items as if they are *fixed*, thereby losing an opportunity to alter the arrangement of the room quickly and easily.

Seating plan

As chairperson, you must be able to make contact with anyone in attendance at any point in the meeting. You will therefore need to be in a central position so that you can see everyone and keep a firm hand on guiding the meeting.

Depending on the shape of the table used, different seating positions allow the chairperson a more dominant impact on the meeting. For instance, if you anticipate conflict, it is helpful to have potential rivals to either side of you rather than facing each other. The following diagrams illustrate a few useful arrangements.

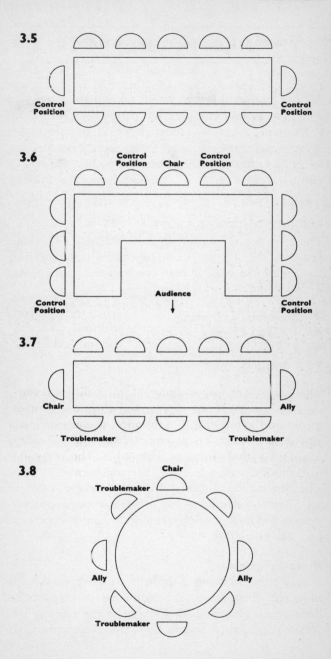

3.5

Control Position

Control Position

3.6

Control Position · Chair · Control Position

Control Position

Control Position

Audience ↓

3.7

Chair

Ally

Troublemaker

Troublemaker

3.8

Chair

Troublemaker

Ally

Ally

Troublemaker

4

THE MEETING IN PROCESS

At any kind of meeting which takes place at regular intervals, certain recognizable patterns of behaviour will become apparent to the chairperson. In order to develop real skills in managing the meeting it is necessary to become attuned to these patterns, as they will exert a good deal of influence over group behaviour and thinking.

UNDERSTANDING GROUPS

The most powerful interests in any meeting – far more powerful than the purported objectives of the meeting itself – are the basic human needs of the participants. These include:

- Economic well-being
- A sense of belonging
- The need for recognition
- Control of one's own life

These needs will be expressed at nearly every point in a meeting, whether or nor participants voice them directly. By recognizing such motivating factors and appealing to people's interests anyone can potentially support, or alternatively undermine, the stated agenda.

The chairperson cannot afford to ignore any such factors as they concern the way in which groups come together, and then develop, around the common perception of a given task.

Group behaviour

A greater appreciation of the behaviour of groups helps both the chairperson and individual participants to understand what is really going on at the meeting. As we all know, what people say is not necessarily what they mean – *how* they say it, and *why* they say it, is often far more significant.

This can be beneficial to the chairperson, in particular:

- Certain phases of group development can be analysed and predicted
- Many of the sources of fruitless conflict can be anticipated and pre-empted

Acceptance and integration

To a greater or lesser extent people are all looking for some identity within a group and a sense of belonging. This applies not only to work situations but also to our roles within a family or social circle.

Anyone entering an established group will be particularly aware of his or her own need for acceptance – hence new arrivals will tend to conform more to existing norms of behaviour within the group, rather than immediately expressing their individuality.

The chairperson's approach

If a new chairperson approaches the meeting determined to impose their views as a palpable show of strength – 'starting as they mean to go on' – they are likely to provoke both resentment and resistance. Whatever their professed indifference to courting popularity, they will soon come to realize that they can achieve very little without a degree of acceptance from the participants.

Newly-established groups

Where the group is newly-established, things tend to develop in a different way. Theoretically *all* participants will be looking to gain acceptance or establish some form of group identity – the starting point, at least, will be the same for everyone. Nevertheless, as different participants engage themselves with varying degrees of effort or effectiveness some may find themselves marginalized while others are more firmly entrenched.

A valuable part of the chairperson's role is to restore some of the balance by drawing members back from the fringes of the group, identifying them and encouraging their involvement.

Communication within the group

More than one meeting has suffered through the assumption that the participants only need information about the matter in hand, rather than about each other. For people to be able to work effectively together it is important that they should be allowed to establish as many areas of common ground as possible. Even social backgrounds or shared interests help to generate understanding and establish points of relationship.

The meeting will particularly benefit from participants' knowledge of their colleagues' experience or areas of expertise – information that may help to foster mutual respect and encourage a more willing acceptance of other people's input.

With effective communication and information sharing, members of the meeting can build stronger relationships, ultimately developing the confidence to share more of their real thoughts and ideas.

Group objectives

An individual participant's objectives provide the sense of purpose which guides their efforts. Group objectives, however, are often more difficult to clarify.

Participants will often have apparently conflicting objectives, or stated group objectives may be little more than a mask for some 'hidden agenda'. Equally, chairpersons may have their own objectives which they seek to impose on the participants.

Uncertainty surrounding objectives, or conflict between them, will have a disastrous effect on the productivity of the meeting. It is vital that everyone, particularly the chairperson, is able to identify and agree on suitable objectives. Without this, the meeting will degenerate into a demotivating free-for-all lacking any co-operation or overall commitment.

Group control

Realistically, any meeting will need some form of control for its objectives to be achieved. The chairperson should ensure that *everyone* is given the chance to contribute.

However, methods of control are likely to inhibit the progress of a meeting if they are either overcomplicated or inflexible:

- **Overcomplicated** – The structure for making proposals or initiating action is so convoluted that sound creative ideas are lost in the process. The ideas that *do* get through are more likely to come from the less imaginative members of the meeting, who are more suited to mastering its structures than tackling the matter in hand.
- **Inflexible** – This will stifle individual input and more or less make redundant the participative framework that a meeting provides. Those members with the most to offer the meeting – in terms of creative problem-solving, for instance – are the most likely to react against it and be demotivated by it.

Another counter-productive effect of *both* of these situations is to allow participants to shift responsibility for action back on to the organizer or chairperson.

Ultimately, if the structure is appropriate to the meeting's aims and content, clearly understood and accepted by the participants, it will lead to effective group work-ing and an appropriate distribution of tasks and authority.

Group development

Primary needs of →	Acceptance →	Communication → (Data Flow)	Objectives → (Goals)	Control
Symptoms if needs are met	Acceptance Confidence Trust	Spontaneity Honest feedback Openness	Creativity Co-operation Commitment	Problem-solving
Symptoms if needs are not met	Fear Suspicion Withdrawal	Polite indifference Hesitant strategy	Apathy Rivalry	Self-appointed leaders

Figure 4.1: Model of Group Development

The chairperson can use this model of group develop-ment (Figure 4.1) in a practical way by asking questions about all of these primary needs – acceptance, com-munication, objectives and control.

Consider, for instance, the following factors:

- What is the level of acceptance, etc. in the group?
- How far are individual needs met?
- What can be done to meet these needs further?

In addition, the chairperson should constantly monitor his or her own meeting group's behaviour for signs of needs met or unfulfilled.

Meeting group needs

Although the action needed to meet all the group's needs will often be impossible to achieve on a practical level, meeting them as far as you can will promote con-structive group behaviour and lead to further develop-ment.

A well-integrated group will be able to tackle the main task more efficiently and successfully than a collection of self-serving individuals pulling in all directions. Each individual member will actually be able to realize more of his or her own potential via a suitably concerted effort. (See Chapter 6 for more detail on participative approaches.)

Group norms

As we have seen, the relative success or failure of a meeting relies almost completely on the interaction between the participants. Like any group of people, they will typically develop in four stages – 'Forming', 'Storming', 'Norming' and 'Performing'.

- **Forming** – The initial coming together of a new group of people and the testing of position and influence.
- **Storming** – The process of disagreeing on such things as values, methods, or simply what the main task is. As previously outlined, it is preferable to bring these differences to the surface, so that they can be confronted and resolved, rather than leave them to fester and recur in the future.
- **Norming** – This is what happens once the members of the group have established workable rules to which the majority subscribe.

The norms, standards or expectations which people demand of one another can vary a great deal from one group to another. Even a group that has never met before will set norms for itself quite quickly.

When a group of people meet for the first time, the initial few minutes of that meeting will most likely set the style and tone for subsequent meetings. Thereafter, those behaviours which conform to the group norm will be rewarded or reinforced, while those which do not will be penalized or discouraged.

It is therefore most important for the chairperson to be familiar with the group norm likely to influence the participants at each of their meetings.

- **Performing** – The fourth, and last, phase of group development. Each group member should be operating to the best of their ability, with rules and agreed methods clear, towards the overall objectives that the group set itself.

TASK AND PROCESS

When any group forms to work on a particular task, there will be various ways of analysing how well people work together and co-operate as a team. Many different behaviour categories can be used. There is a clear difference, for example, between:

Task behaviours – which emphasize the content of work, and
Process behaviours – which emphasize how people relate to one another and work together

Examples of task behaviours

- **Initiating** – Suggesting ideas or putting forward new definitions of the problem:

  'I suggest that we discuss the situation in the maintenance plant before we look at what caused the fire.'

- **Building** – Seeking to develop or extend a proposal which has been made by someone else:

  'So if we discuss the maintenance plant, we could link up the three previous suggestions about fire prevention and form a new procedure by the end of the discussion.'

Examples of process behaviours

- **Gate-keeping** – Making sure every member of the meeting is able to contribute:

  'Joe has not said anything so far, and I know that he has some previous experience of this problem.'

- **Expressing feelings** – Summarizing the way the meeting is progressing and the reactions of individuals:

  'I think we are all a bit disappointed with our discussion on item three, but are happy overall with the way that we have agreed on the other items.'

Key behaviour skills of the successful chairperson
There is a tendency, at meetings, to become 'task-mesmerized' and ignore how the group is actually working together. The chairperson should try to counteract this tendency and focus on the processes of the meeting – the *how* rather than the *what*.

Research has shown that the effective chairperson avoids making proposals on the content of the meeting but does make a large number of procedural proposals – again, *how* to achieve rather than *what* to achieve.

A SEQUENCE OF DECISION MAKING
Decisions normally need to be taken before the end of each meeting, with a view to subsequent action being implemented. The chairperson's role involves steering the discussion towards a point at which suitable action can be agreed. At the same time, encouraging the maximum possible contribution from all those present.

Seek agreement on the basic issues or problems to be discussed
Define them for everyone at the meeting, but avoid presenting such problems as if they are *passive* ones, for instance:

'. . . the house is burning down!'

Instead, the problems should be portrayed as *active*, encouraging people's involvement:

'. . . how are we going to put out the fire?'

Separate problems into a number of categories, and decide the sequence of discussing them
Going through each element in turn will prevent you from being defeated by the scale of the overall problem.

Put forward the facts about this newly-defined problem
Be careful to distinguish between accepted 'data' (which is not to be challenged in any way), and judgments or opinions (generally a reflection of people's preferences and prejudices).

Now allow the meeting to discuss their interpretation of the basic data already agreed
It is at this point that any personal prejudices, opinions, or vested interests can be most obvious.

Now move on to considering alternative courses of possible action
These arise from the participants' own interpretations of the problem

Decide on different courses of action
Participants' own criteria for taking a decision and what the potential advantages and disadvantages might be.

Ensure that someone is made responsible for taking follow-up action on the decision
Their name should be recorded in the minutes. The results of their actions can then form the basis for any further meetings on the subject.

5

THE SKILLS OF THE CHAIRPERSON

The chairperson's role is to guide the meeting via a care-fully-constructed agenda. He or she must be sensitive to the motivations and feelings of the participants, able to draw out any positive contributions and curb any negative input.

All participants also have power to influence decisions at meetings, power that is often left untapped. It is up to the chairperson to harness this – encouraging contributions from the reticent, stemming the flow of the garrulous and keeping everyone to the point.

Tasks of the chairperson
These can be split up into six general categories:

- Getting the meeting under way
- Guiding the meeting on through each successive stage, by way of the agenda
- Summarizing each stage before moving on – thereby unequivocally establishing what has been the agreed course of action
- Ensuring a written record is kept of all mutual decisions and agreed action – this can then be referred back to as an aid to later meetings
- Guiding the meeting away from detrimental areas of conflict, back on to areas of common ground as a basis for discussion
- Ensuring that all participants have the opportunity to contribute to the meeting

APPROACHING THE MEETING

'The first act'

The chairperson must first open the meeting in an appropriate way. As ever, first impressions are disproportionately important! The way that you, as chairperson, start the meeting will probably have an enormous impact on how your input will be received and how people will react to you during the course of the meeting.

It is only by considering the individual needs, wants and motivations of the other participants that you will be able to tailor your approach to the demands of the situation.

Presentation

Remember, what you actually say is only a part of the impression you give to others. People will pay equal attention to your tone of voice, facial expression and general body language.

Everything you do, much of it non-verbal behaviour, will communicate itself to your audience, the other participants in the meeting. If your mood is cheerful and optimistic, you will send a positive signal to them. Conversely, should you seem pessimistic or generally unenthusiastic this is bound to have a demotivating effect on the whole meeting.

Chairperson's preparation

Well before the meeting, you should give careful consideration to the actual process that is to take place – forewarned is forearmed! Obviously the clearer an idea you have of the desired outcome, the better able you will be to respond appropriately during the meeting.

When you come to prepare, therefore, take the following into consideration:

- What do you want to have achieved by the end of the meeting?
- Who will be in attendance?
- What do *they* want to have achieved by the end of the meeting?
- What are their roles in relation to you?
- What kind of prejudices or preconceptions do they bring with them, and how might these affect their role at the meeting?
- What shared ideas or philosophies do you all have that could form common ground in the meeting?
- What could you say or do to emphasize these areas of common ground – particularly at the outset of the meeting?

All these questions will guide you to a greater understanding of the participants and their likely role. This can also help you to identify areas of which you are not fully aware where you require greater knowledge or understanding, giving you enough time for further research.

From the outset you need not only to get the attention of the participants, but also make them all feel that *they* can contribute. Wit and humour may help, if you feel comfortable with that style, although an enforced jocular style is more likely to arouse suspicion than anything else.

Even if you feel unable to use a joke convincingly to put people at their ease, it is good practice to plan a remark that could 'break the ice' in some way – and hopefully points to some sort of common bond. This helps the participants to relate to you in a way they might not have anticipated before the meeting.

With your entire approach, apparent confidence is of key importance. As chairperson, you should look and sound as though you expect the meeting to achieve its objectives easily – sometimes quite a challenge!

Establish objectives

In the early stages it is important that you state clearly the main purpose of the meeting, and give some idea of its intended structure. Provide an overview of the subject, or issues involved, and introduce any relevant experts or specialists who have been brought in to participate.

These early remarks should be made as clear as possible to set the meeting off in the right direction. You may find it useful to write them down and rehearse them a few times, so that you will be able to put them across effectively at the actual meeting.

Establish time-scales

From the outset establish the time-scale of the meeting, and the relative time allocated to each area of discussion. State when you expect the meeting to finish. This prevents participants from assuming that the discussion is an open-ended one, giving them free rein to digress into areas of indulgent self-interest.

Consider others

It is important that you develop a good understanding of the participants and their interests. Appealing to these interests may, at some point, mean getting the meeting finished as soon as possible! Even this is legitimate if it means that the participants are encouraged to make the best use of the time there is.

You should be able to communicate on a level that they will readily understand – saying what needs to be said and avoiding areas of needless conflict.

Stimulate discussion

Present items simply and concisely in a firm, confident manner. Aim to introduce a topic in such a way that you stimulate discussion from a number of different perspectives. Where someone appears reticent, or disinclined to offer an opinion, try to build their confidence and draw them into the discussion: 'Well, Michael, what's your perspective on this?'

Limit conflict
When dealing with contentious issues where there is likely to be conflict between participants, try to limit the debate by suggesting boundaries as to what is discussed.

Expect the unexpected
Along with all the things that you, as chairperson, *can* plan ahead for are those circumstances which are unavoidably out of your control. Hence you will need to take into account both late arrivals and early departures, minimizing any detrimental effect they may have on the flow of the meeting.

STRUCTURING THE MEETING
It is your job, as chairperson, to structure the meeting – making the best use of the time available, to obtain the desired outcome. Different types of meeting will require different styles and methods of control.

Even between one item on an agenda and another you may be required to modify your approach to an appreciable extent, balancing the need to allow free-flowing discussion with the constraints of time. While defining strict limits as to who speaks, how they speak, and for how long you must also create the opportunity for active contributions from all present.

Use background information
For each item on the agenda you should provide background information – as to previously agreed courses of action etc. – which provides both context and perspective for discussion of the current situation. This will

give participants a better idea of what is required, and could prevent a duplication of effort by highlighting avenues already explored.

Encourage controlled discussion

The next step is to stimulate discussion from several points of view. This is obviously important, as the reason for having a meeting, rather than issuing a directive or memo, is to encourage discussion from a variety of perspectives. All the while, however, you must keep things within the structure of the agenda – in order to prevent the meeting degenerating into a personal confrontation.

The same control must apply to the time allowed for each topic. Although you need to give the participants a certain amount of time to explore the issues involved, if they are left for too long they will lose focus, perhaps become bored, and drift into inconsequential side issues.

SUMMARIZING

This is an important skill for the chairperson to acquire. It can be used for a number of purposes at different stages of the meeting.

- As a signal to a participant that they have 'had their say' and that it may be time to allow another member of the meeting to speak
- To signal the end of one phase of the discussion or form the basis of another
- To bring together the disparate strands of the discussion – particularly where this has rambled on for some time and you need to draw together a series of complicated arguments
- To gauge the degree of real agreement that exists over a particular decision
- To clarify exactly *what* has been agreed

- *To confirm agreed action*
- To help the meeting secretary write accurate, and therefore useful, minutes

CONTROL

The chairperson needs to strike a fine balance between two quite different aspects of control: procedural control and process control.

control

- Stick to the agenda
- Keep to time
- Keep the discussion on the issue at hand
- Make decisions
- Agree actions

These are all good solid requirements that might lead you to believe that a chairperson must rule with the proverbial 'rod of iron'. Nevertheless, the following should also be borne in mind.

Process control

At the same time as fulfilling those rather stringent requirements the chairperson must also ensure that everyone present has an opportunity to air his or her views. For this to happen the chairperson must:

- Facilitate discussion
- Involve all participants
- Encourage different views and perspectives
- Allow extensive debate on those items that warrant it
- Encourage creativity

Remember – It is precisely *because* there is a framework and a degree of 'discipline' that everyone will have a chance to contribute.

FACILITATING DISCUSSION

The skills involved in facilitating discussion can be broken down and learnt in the following way.

Listening

This means not only the verbal content, what someone actually says at a meeting, but also the range of non-verbal messages that are communicated at the same time, including:

- The actual feeling behind the message
- The tone and pitch of the voice
- The things that *aren't* said
- The posture and facial expression

Listening in this way can be a demanding process. To do it successfully you will need to concentrate hard and pay a good deal of attention to whoever is speaking.

Dealing with 'difficult' participants

In any group of people there are bound to be a few that you, as chairperson, find difficult to control in an appropriate way.

- The person who talks too much
- The person who wants an immediate decision on everything
- The person who makes dogmatic statements
- The person who takes up personal 'duels' with other people
- The person who is inattentive, whispering incessantly, or simply not listening

In dealing with such participants you should de-personalize the issue away from them, usually with questions which refer the problem back to group opinion:

- 'Does the group feel we are making progress?'

- Do you think your approach will really help us to reach a solution?'

Quite often you can bring the discussion back into focus by merely restating the topic. At other times a pause in progress may be desirable to allow the airing of feelings, or for exploratory discussion. Allowing participants to get certain things out of their system may sometimes be the only way for the meeting eventually to progress.

DIFFICULT SITUATIONS

Someone extends the discussion beyond the topic as outlined by the chairperson
The chairperson should intervene and explain that the discussion is drifting away from the matter at hand:

> 'Yes, Jane. What you're saying *is* interesting, but the agreed item now is to decide alternatives . . .'

Someone becomes muddled and confused
The chairperson must be supportive, coaxing the participant to re-state the point more explicitly:

> 'My understanding is that you think we should . . .'

Someone rambles at great length
The chairperson must intervene to save the meeting's valuable time. Nevertheless, this should be done in a sensitive and supportive way:

> 'I think we all take your point on that issue, but another perspective can only help. Should we hear what Alison has to say?'

Someone habitually makes vague suggestions
The chairperson must clarify these suggestions before allowing the discussion to proceed:

'Could you be a little more specific? What sort of scheme do you have in mind, and when would it start?'

Someone habitually interrupts other participants while they are speaking

This may be acceptable if the speaker is being corrected on a factual error. Similarly, a humorous interjection may be useful in keeping the discussion on friendly, co-operative terms. If not, then the chairperson must keep control of who speaks, and when:

'Could we have your point after Tony has finished speaking, he may answer it for you if he's allowed to continue . . .'

Someone persists in chatting to their neighbour

The chairperson needs to draw attention to the matter in hand and encourage everyone to pay attention. A direct question can be effective in keeping people listening actively:

'Could I just check your thoughts on Joanna's last point, Brian?'

General guidelines

As a chairperson, your skills in dealing with awkward people – or the resultant awkward situations – are important in adequately fulfilling that role. Some general guidelines are helpful:

- Accept people as they are
- Stay in the present, don't dwell on the past
- Treat people individually – taking in to account their personality – in order to treat them equally
- Trust others, even if you feel there is a risk in doing so
- Do not rely on constant approval – achieving popularity is not a primary objective!

IMPROVING PARTICIPATION

So far an assumption has been made that the role of the chairperson is to control the meeting, in a positive and constructive fashion. A more informal style of control is required, however, when the meeting's purpose is to solve a problem or learn something new. Here, participants should be enabled to take on more responsibility for the meeting's outcome by sharing the role of chairperson or facilitator.

CHAIRPERSON AS FACILITATOR

The facilitator role
The term 'facilitator' is used in this book to refer to the person who enables individuals in a group or meeting to learn and develop their potential by focusing on the ways in which they interact with each other.

In order to run a more participative meeting, the chairperson has to use many of the skills of the facilitator. For example, conflict is always with us – instead of smoothing over, ignoring or compromising in the face of it, the meeting can directly confront conflict. Its resolution will result in increased commitment to working together by everybody involved.

Open communications
For a team meeting to be successful the participants must feel able to discuss and criticize each others' suggestions without feeling threatened. They need to cultivate the skill of open communications.

When holding a problem-solving meeting with your subordinates, it is not advisable to begin by stating your own preferences. This will discourage your team from expressing their views.

A better strategy is first to find out whether the team shares your understanding of the problem. Once this has been established the facilitator can both invite and encourage their ideas and solutions.

Competitiveness and individualism initially appear threats to co-operation and teamworking, but the manner in which these instincts are channelled and directed will determine their influence, be it positive or negative. There must be a foundation of mutual trust and respect between participants before participative processes can have the desired effects.

Skills of the facilitator

- **Create a climate of support and openness within the group**

  Participants feel safe enough to contribute fully and freely to the meeting.

- **Encourage participants to express their feelings and contribute their ideas**

  Help those present to feel they belong to the team. Involvement in discussion, contribution of ideas and arriving at group decisions generate a feeling of ownership and commitment to those decisions on the part of the participant. Ideally the end result should be greater than the sum of the participants! This concept (put simply, $2+2=5$) is known as 'synergy'.

- **Encourage active participation and share the leadership role**

  Over a period of time team members can be led by a skilful facilitator to appreciate that each person has some expertise they can contribute to the meeting and to give them the opportunity to do so.

EFFECTIVE GROUPS

Research into group behaviour has shown that complete control and manipulation of a group by a so-called expert is very difficult and largely self-defeating. The well organized and well integrated group can be very successful – decision making, organizing and functioning responsibly.

The results of this research show that the characteristics of the effective group, as opposed to the ineffective group, are shown in Figure 6.1.

Characteristic	Effective Group	Ineffective Group
Atmosphere	Informal, relaxed; all members involved and interested	Formal, tense, undercurrents of indifference
Discussion	Everyone contributes with relevance to task	Dominated by a few; often irrelevant
Objectives	Formulated by all members – understood and accepted	Not clearly defined, individuals have private aims
Listening	Everyone prepared to listen – members put forward their own views	Poor, often responding to irrelevant matters
Disagreements	Careful attempts at resolution	Suppressed or open conflict – aggressive sub-group
Decisions	General consensus but individuals free to disagree	No systematic discussion of method
Criticism	Seen as constructive, welcomed	Destructive
Feelings	People free to express their feelings	Kept hidden under the surface
Actions	Clear and understood	Not clearly defined
Chairperson	Leadership role shifts to appropriate person	Dominates group
Review process	Frequent review	Not done

Figure 6.1: Characteristics of effective and ineffective groups

The need for change

Regular and routine meetings can become little more than social events, with no decisions being made and virtually no resultant change in business practices or relationships.

> *If you always do what you've always done*
> *You'll always get what you've always got!*

If this is your situation, you need to make a change to a more participative style of meeting. The following three sections illustrate some alternatives worth considering.

DECISION-MAKING BY CONSENSUS

A creative role for the facilitator

Consensus is the process of reaching agreement on any subject under discussion without taking a vote – achieving it can certainly be quite a challenge for all those involved. Nevertheless, it represents an important process for drawing participants into a co-operative approach to problem-solving.

A fundamental requirement is for participants to view differences of opinion as being helpful, rather than destructive – a means of establishing areas of difficulty with a view to overcoming them.

Establishing resources or expertise

The facilitator must look closely at the requirements of the task at hand and ensure that everyone is clear on the overall objectives. Anyone within the meeting who has special expertise or relevant knowledge should be identified and utilized. The facilitator can establish who they might be by asking simple, open-ended questions:

- 'Does anyone here have any special knowledge of this problem?'

- 'Have any of you done this sort of thing before?'

This process of acknowledging and involving those with relevant expertise serves two purposes. First, it is obviously useful in achieving an optimum resolution of the issues involved. Second, it uses people's skills in a constructive and participative way – sharing out areas of leadership with those who obviously have most to contribute. Possible conflict about who is the most empowered to recommend solutions is avoided as people's strengths and expertise will have already been acknowledged.

The facilitator must also establish a baseline of knowledge, assumption and understanding about the task. The most easy way to do this is, again, to ask questions. Any technical terms or jargon need to be clarified so that all the participants will be able to make a contribution couched in their own terms.

Avoiding or resolving conflict

Areas of possible conflict should be identified by the facilitator, who should attempt to draw them out into the open and overcome them. Then, at least, the participants involved will feel that they have had a fair hearing with their points of view understood – if not supported – by their colleagues. This approach aims to remove any feelings of resentment or anger that may affect participants' contributions to the meeting.

Facilitator's checklist

For the meeting to be effective it is important for the facilitator to preserve the flexibility of the procedure – even monitoring their own role to ensure that *they* are influencing rather than contributing. The facilitator must, therefore, keep the following in mind:

- Is the task understood?

- Are expertise and resources identified and shared?
- Are assumptions and knowledge commonly shared?
- Is a co-operative atmosphere established?
- Have everyone's views been expressed and understood?
- Is there consensus at each successive stage?
- Has any undue influence on the facilitator's part been minimized?

THE NEGOTIATED AGENDA

The following guidelines represent a fairly radical rethink of some of the traditional meeting processes. In practice, however, they have proved most effective in a number of settings.

- The agenda is constructed at the outset of the meeting. Participants may add items if they can justify their relevance to the rest of the meeting.
- A separate facilitator is chosen by the meeting for each agenda item.
- Minutes are written as the meeting progresses and recorded, on a flipchart for instance, for all to refer to.
- Each item on the agenda is 'owned' by one of the participants, hence he or she will usually become facilitator for that topic.
- The purpose of any agenda item is explicit – e.g. information-giving, problem-solving – and must be justified by the participant who suggested it.
- The time allotted to each agenda is pre-set, so that participants can establish the degree of urgency relevant to particular areas.

At the heart of this meetings process is the conscious use of time, the setting of priorities and the establishing of clearly-defined roles at the meeting. In one work situation where these procedures have been introduced, the time spent in routine meetings has dropped by a third.

THE 'ONE GOAL' APPROACH

This approach is most useful if the meeting is primarily to increase the skills of the participants. The term 'learning community' has been used to sum up both the intention and the method. It is especially useful where the meeting is one where the objective is a sharing of ideas or complementary skills.

ONE – Establishing the role of participants

Offers – to make to the meeting
Needs – from that meeting
End result – that is expected by the end of the meeting

The facilitator opens the meeting by explaining that the agenda is to be negotiated and agreed by the participants. Each of them is invited to introduce themselves and outline their experience, stating in simple terms:

- What they can **offer** or contribute to the meeting
- What they specifically **need** from the meeting
- What particular **end result** they are looking for

The facilitator can then write up these ideas, perhaps on a flipchart, so that all of the participants have a clear overview of each other's approach to the meeting.

GOA . . . L – Negotiating the agenda

Get
Others'
Agreement

This involves establishing the agenda by mutual consent, where possible agreeing the timing as well as the sequence of the topics or issues. The facilitator should carefully observe participants' *non-verbal* reactions, to assess where areas of disagreement may arise.

Limit discussion

Having guided the participant to agreement on the agenda and the desired end results, the facilitator can now limit the discussion to the areas to which everyone has been able to contribute. Where participants drift away from the main points the facilitator will be able to draw them back to the point with the implied consent of all concerned. This process is valuable in focusing everyone on the matters in hand.

PARTICIPATION, PRESENTATION AND INFLUENCING SKILLS

This chapter is a complex one. So far we have concentrated on the chairperson as the primary source of influence in the meeting. Now we look at ways in which each individual taking part can contribute most effectively.

We also consider *presentation skills* – how to make your point clearly and with maximum impact. Then we look at *influencing skills* – using your understanding of the meeting and its members to act as a 'vice–chairperson', inspiring constructive discussion and discouraging inappropriate behaviour amongst your colleagues.

EFFECTIVE PARTICIPATION

Be prepared
Preparation is vital. Spend as much time as possible becoming familiar with the background to any meeting you attend:

- Are there any papers or minutes which you should read and absorb?
- Who will be there?
- What sort of common ground will there be between you and the other participants?
- How can you go about establishing shared interests before the meeting?

Be prompt
Make sure you know exactly where the meeting is being held and leave enough time to get there. Don't let yourself be distracted by last-minute telephone calls or

conversations. Being late will put you at an immediate disadvantage – not only will you appear disorganized to the other participants but you may have missed important information. You could then spend the rest of the meeting frantically trying to catch up, potentially missing further relevant points in the process.

Be alert

Do adopt a positive and alert posture during the meeting. *Don't* do the following:

- Stare off into space
- Slouch
- Fidget
- Look as though you are merely paying lip-service to somebody's opinions while you wait for *your* say

By your approach you should convey to the other members of the meeting that you are really paying attention, concentrating hard on what other people are saying. Then, when you come to speak, they will naturally listen more attentively to your views if they feel you have given them a fair hearing.

Be positive

Always look for what's positive about the meeting or what someone is saying – rather than focusing on what's negative, or allowing your personal antipathy towards a colleague to make you dismiss their comments out of hand. If your reservations are justified, they will be more convincingly put across through a reasoned approach than by resorting to dogma or obvious prejudice.

Be involved

Do seek to be the kind of participant you would expect others to be. The more attention you pay, and the more you are seen to pay:

- The more you will get out of the meeting
- The more the meeting will reflect positively on you and your professional approach

GENERAL PRESENTATION SKILLS

It is a natural tendency to assume that everything you say at the meeting will be interpreted in precisely the positive way that you want it to be by everyone else present. Unfortunately the potential for misunderstanding and misinterpretation is considerable.

Preparation and care in the way you present yourself at meetings is important if you really want to be heard and be a part of facilitating change.

Timing

It is often an irresistible temptation to introduce ideas or opinions into the meeting as soon as they occur to you. Not only is this likely to disrupt the flow of the discussion, it may also mean that perfectly valid ideas are stillborn through being introduced before their natural time. An effective participant will time his or her contributions for the point in the meeting where they are most appropriate.

Judgment

A key skill is that of being able to listen carefully to the discussion and judge the stage the meeting is at any particular time. Each agenda item can go through a cycle of phases such as:

- Defining the problem
- Collecting information
- Defining the next step
- Taking action
- Analysing what happened
- Drawing out principles for potential future use

Signal your attention

When you feel that the time *is* appropriate for you to make a point, you should try to lead into it in some way, so that you have engaged the meeting's attention before you reach the crux of the matter, for instance:

> 'I'd like to ask a question about . . .'

This effectively signals your intention. Once your 'audience' is listening you can be sure they will absorb most of what you are saying, rather than missing the first sentence or so through being taken unawares. You will also have gained a little extra time to compose your thoughts, should you need it.

MAKING A FORMAL PRESENTATION

At some time or other you may find yourself required to make a formal presentation of some kind at a meeting. Whether this takes less than two minutes, or over half an hour, certain principles remain the same. The following three steps will make your presentation more effective:

- **Plan** what you want to say, to whom and when
- **Prepare** how you propose to say it, including use of visual aids
- **Practise** – i.e. rehearse before the event with a 'walk-through' (or maybe 'stagger-through') of the presentation. Better to identify and overcome problems at this stage than on the day

Planning

There are three key elements to consider all at once for effective planning, which can be summed up by the mnemonic 'OAC'.

'O' for Outcome/Objectives – What are you hoping to have achieved by the end of the presentation? It is useful to imagine people's likely reactions to what you say and, more importantly, how you say it.

'A' for Audience – Who is the presentation aimed at?

You can develop a summary by considering another three 'A's.

- **Aims** – What sort of aims will the audience have in listening to you? Will they be more interested in short- or long-term implications? Are there any vested interests? Are you likely to get a fair hearing?
- **Aspirations/Ambitions** – What do they hope to achieve, and what efforts are they prepared to make in that direction? What suggested outcomes will most appeal to them?
- **Assumptions** – Are they likely to have any preconceptions about you and your role? May they even be suspicious of your motives? Even if you are not particularly familiar with the other participants you may be able to get some clues to their attitudes by speaking with their colleagues or associates beforehand.

By following this process you should gain a clearer understanding of the people to whom your presentation will be directed. This will not only help you to assess what they will respond to, but also help you to identify possible sticking points and take pre-emptive action.

'C' for Content – How will your planning of the outcome and your understanding of the audience affect the content of your presentation? Once you have established the content, you may need to reassess your expectations of the outcome or, perhaps, ask further questions about your audience.

OAC is often not a straightforward progress from *Outcome* to *Audience* to *Content* – you may find yourself repeating steps or going back and forth from one to another to achieve an optimum result.

Preparation
You can now start to plan the way in which you will present the ideas or information that you need to put

across. Your presentation must gain the attention of your audience from the outset, giving them an overview of what you are going to say, and if necessary telling them what sort of involvement you expect from them – when they can ask questions, for example.

A useful tip is to prepare the first few sentences carefully, to gain maximum impact. Every audience will give you at least 30 seconds at the start – while they make up their minds whether they want to pay attention to what you have to say.

It will help if you can start by outlining how many key points you are going to make. You can then use this number as a 'map' of the presentation, for example:

> 'Now I've finished with the third point we can concentrate on the fourth, which is quite controversial.'

Good presentations should leave people inspired, motivated and empowered to act effectively on what has been decided. If you can find a suitably positive or encouraging note to end on – one which will mean something to that particular audience – you are more likely to engage them in achieving the stated objectives.

Rehearsal

The amount of rehearsal that you need to devote to a presentation will obviously depend on your familiarity with the subject and the complexity of the content. It is possible, however, to *over-rehearse* – which will result in a rather stiff, laboured presentation.

Although it is important to know your subject thoroughly, your prepared material should really only be a series of key points – leaving adequate room for you to put them across with a degree of spontaneity.

Over-preparation leaves little or no scope for useful variations or digressions.

Persuasion

If the objective of the presentation is to persuade the participants to follow a particular course of action or adopt a particular approach it is as well to start with an acknowledgement of all their likely objections. Unless such negative points are brought out into the open, the participants will not accept that you have really under-stood their point of view. Facing such objections head on will at least give your proposals a degree of credibility, and also provide you with the opportunity to take pre-emptive action.

Aims to inform	Aims to persuade
* Give an overview of your (5) points then signal them as you introduce each one	* State proposition * Acknowledge possible objections
1. _____ 2. _____ 3. _____ 4. _____ 5. _____	1. _____ 2. _____ (etc.)
* Summarize the (5) points	* Now state positive advantages or benefits of your proposition
	1. _____ 2. _____ (etc.)
Tell them what you're going to tell them Then actually tell them Then tell them what you've told them	Create a vision of life after the outcome has been achieved – showing the benefits it will bring them

Figure 7.1: Different presentation aims and their structures

Pacing yourself

Getting the timing right can be a critical factor at meetings. Over-running may make it appear that you have been 'waffling', whereas 'drying up' after only a quarter of your allotted time can make you look incompetent or ill-prepared. Of these two faults, the most common is for people to include too much material and over-run. It is also worth leaving adequate time for discussion or question and answer sessions, where appropriate.

PRESENTATION SKILLS

Basically, your most important technique is being yourself. No specific 'trick' or technique will be effective unless you have integrated it into your own personal style. Sincerity and enthusiasm are infectious and will always come across to your audience. They will more readily identify with these characteristics than any amount of high-flown theory or technique.

By being yourself you are creating an honest and open approach that will make your audience far more ready to trust you, or feel some affinity with your opinions. Also, as we have already seen, if you know enough about them to understand their attitudes and perceptions you will be able to present things in a manner to which they can readily relate.

Eye contact

The more directly that you look at the members of your audience, the more likely you are to build some sort of rapport. Eye-to-eye contact can be a most successful way of putting across self-assurance (if you are not sure of what you are saying, they certainly are unlikely to be swayed by it) and honesty (such a direct approach signifies that you have nothing to hide).

In the context of a large meeting it will obviously be impossible for you to establish eye contact with *everyone* present. Nevertheless, remember that it should *not* be limited to looking at:

- An unspecified area six inches above everyone's head

- Your notes or, in extreme cases, your shoes
- The most influential person in the meeting
- The most friendly face in the meeting

Appearance

In the early stages of a presentation your appearance will be crucial to your credibility. As with most other things, your audience will all have different expectations about dress and draw their own inference as to what it signifies. What one person sees as a smart, obviously authoritative figure, another will see as a stiff-collared busybody with no conception of life at the 'sharp end' of the company.

Where you are working in an unfamiliar setting, therefore, it is prudent to find out something about the dress code for the meeting. Being smartly dressed is generally good policy, but being appropriately dressed for your audience and location is more important.

INFLUENCING SKILLS

To influence the meeting you must first acknowledge the role of the psychological and political undercurrents which may be present – then the techniques and manoeuvres used to exploit them. The following are examples of some of the most common ways in which people seek to influence meetings.

Keeping key business away from a particular meeting

This well-known tactic is often used when someone believes their idea will be opposed or even defeated if submitted to a meeting. Major items are fixed beforehand, the meeting itself is a sham and the minutes are doctored for public consumption.

Alternatively, an item can be kept from successive meetings until becomes it too late to find an alternative.

Lobbying

Successful influencing can begin well before the meeting itself. Analyse previous trends, interests, how power is exercised and by whom, and outcomes. You can then ascertain support for a contentious item before it comes under discussion.

Recognition of power

Some or all of the sources of power identified below may be at work in any meeting. Understanding them and how they affect participants' behaviour is a necessary skill for anyone seeking to be more influential at meetings.

- **Expert power** – Is conferred on people thought to have specialist knowledge. The important point to remember is that their power depends, not necessarily on their actual knowledge, but on the perceptions of other people.
- **Reward power** – Exists when an individual has the power to reward someone else for compliance with their instructions. The reward may be money, promotion, responsibility or support for a chosen course of action.
- **Coercion power** – Almost the reverse of reward power, it is the ability to punish by withdrawal of favours, friendship or emotional support.
- **Reference power** – Otherwise known as power through charisma or personality. This individual can inspire and persuade others to comply with their wishes.

The 'hidden' agenda

The hidden agenda consists of issues that are not on the agenda, which concern the participants as much as, or more than, those issues which are. The hidden agenda will rarely be overtly discussed at the meeting, although it will influence the way it is conducted and the participants' behaviour.

Participants under a threat of redundancy, for instance,

will not behave objectively – they will not be honest and they will be suspicious of one another. Upon the removal of the threat people will again be able to trust each other and this particular hidden agenda will vanish.

Other forms of coercion

Pressure put on some participants by their colleagues, in order to secure a particular outcome, is another manifestation of the hidden agenda. To dispel it, identify the strategies in use and confront the perpetrators with what is actually going on. Banish the element of secrecy so that the issues can be discussed in an open and positive way.

STEERING THE MEETING

Everyone has the potential to influence the meeting, irrespective of their role. There is no reason why the chairperson should take all the initiatives or do all the work.

Anyone can steer the meeting by being aware of its processes. Are the participants listening, giving their full attention to the topic, or arguing? If the chairperson does not or cannot intervene, there are a number of approaches you can take yourself.

- **Bringing in** – Invite an opinion from someone who is not being given an opportunity to contribute:

    'You have not spoken so far, Jenny, what would you like to say on this proposal?'

- **Relieving tension** – Restore a sense of proportion or add a touch of humour:

    'If the competition could see us now, they'd have a good laugh!'

- **Mediating** – Acknowledge and reconcile other people's views:

  'Colin and John clearly want the same outcome for the department, but probably by using different methods. Perhaps they could each explain the advantages of their own proposals.'

- **Summarizing** – Remind people of the stage they have reached:

  'It seems to me that the last five minutes have brought forward three new ideas that need to be considered as follows . . .'

- **Dramatic movements** – Stand up abruptly, knocking back your chair. You now have (hopefully) gained the meeting's attention and have the opportunity to remind them of their real objective:

  'What are we trying to achieve at present?'

- **Increase the irrelevancies** – In the face of increasingly irrelevant debate exaggerate the flow by making progressively more meaningless remarks until it becomes obvious to all concerned. This is an ideal point for you to ask:

  'What are we here for, anyway?'

- **Leaving quietly** – Effective when there is an argument between two or more people to no particular purpose. Without saying anything at all, get up and quietly leave. When you next see the people concerned you can explain why you behaved as you did, or you can pointedly remind participants that if the same thing happens again you have no intention of staying.

- **'Ten minutes more'** – Announce in a loud voice that you have 'only ten more minutes' before you have to leave, ask: 'What are we hoping to achieve in that time?' Make sure you do leave once the time is up.

These interventions are designed to gain the meeting's attention in an unusual way, with the purpose of steering it in a different direction. A lot depends on how accurately you assess the mood of the meeting and how dramatically you perform.

REVIEW AND FOLLOW UP

Very few organizations take the trouble to work out the actual cost of their meetings. For instance, bringing to-gether senior managers for protracted periods of time can prove surprisingly expensive, merely in terms of salary – not to mention the background planning and preparation necessary. For more prestigious meetings there could well be travel, hotel and conferencing expenses to take into account as well.

The immediate financial demands are relatively simple to quantify. More difficult to calculate, however, is the effectiveness of the meeting in improving efficiency or productivity for the future. Remember that if you waste time, you also waste money.

The follow-up steps described below are designed to provide ways to evaluate the number and type of meet-ings you hold, with the intention of streamlining the process, holding fewer, more effective meetings and consequently running a more motivated, cost-effective operation.

INDIVIDUAL MEETING REVIEW

At the end of each individual meeting allocate a short period for each participant to comment on how the meeting was run, and suggest possible improvements. Attentive listening and careful recording is important for this approach, so that small – but potentially signifi-cant – changes are acknowledged and acted upon.

Extend this approach by encouraging participants to write down their thoughts and forward them to the chairperson, or whoever is running the review proce-dure. A few simple questions are enough to yield worthwhile results:

- How clear were the objectives of the meeting?
- Was the agenda made available in good time?
- How satisfied were you with the outcome of the meeting?

For clarity and ease of use, it may be useful for the answers to be graded on a scale, for instance:

NOT AT
ALL..1..2..3..4..5..6..7..8..9..COMPLETELY

When this procedure has been in place for a while – and if it seems to be yielding useful results – think about introducing more difficult types of question with more illuminating results. For instance:

- How helpful was the chairperson in handling the agenda?

Clearly, this requires a chairperson who is prepared to consider potentially critical comments about their performance.

Develop written feedback still further via the inclusion of a number of open-ended questions. Utilizing, as they do, participants' personal thoughts, these could give a deeper insight into those factors which are preventing the meeting from functioning satisfactorily, for instance asking:

- What, in your view, are the major factors which prevent the meeting from being more effective?

MEETINGS REVIEW PROCEDURE
The following questionnaire is to be completed by all the participants at the meeting. A total number of marks for each item is added up to represent the overall rating from everyone in attendance. Items with the

lowest scores can then be discussed and action agreed on as to how to improve the meeting in these areas.

Meeting review sheet (each item to be marked out of 10)

(1) Are our meeting necessary?
(2) Are our meetings useful?
(3) Do we meet at the right frequency?
(4) Are our meetings the right length?
(5) Are our meetings at the right time?
(6) Do the right people attend?
(7) Are our agendas appropriate?
(8) Do we have the necessary information?
(9) Do we have effective decision-making procedures?
(10) Do we make the right use of external help?
(11) Is our meeting room adequate?
(12) Do we use appropriate aids?
(13) Do we keep appropriate records?
(14) Is timekeeping satisfactory?
(15) Are potential interruptions handled correctly?
(16) Are refreshment arrangements adequate?
(17) Is the room laid out correctly?
(18) Do we review our performance effectively?
(19) Do we learn from our mistakes?
(20) Do we take action as a result of performance reviews?

THE MEETINGS AUDIT

Just as any organization carries out a financial audit, a similar procedure can be applied to examine the number and type of meetings held. It is then possible to assess whether the time and effort – and therefore money – currently devoted to organizing and attending meetings is justified. Are the meetings a cost-effective process to achieve the desired outcomes?

The auditing process is made up of a sequence of three stages:

Types and number of meetings
This information may require some investigation as informal (unrecorded) meetings can easily arise. An attempt should be made to classify the nature and purpose of each meeting.

Aims, objectives and outcomes
What kind of meetings (staff, policy, board etc.) are they? What are their aims and objectives? Are these aims and objectives sufficiently communicated to everyone who attends? It is useful to devise a simple questionnaire to gauge participants' individual reactions.

Evaluating their effectiveness
Once the objectives of each meeting have been clarified, their actual outcomes can be used to form a relative view of their success. Where it becomes apparent that meetings have fallen some way short of achieving their objectives you should take steps to find out why. Again, it can be useful to devise a simple questionnaire to assess individual reactions. Did the right people go to the meeting? Who was left out, and in what areas did this create a deficiency or imbalance? Where there were personality clashes could these have been avoided with more careful preparation or a more perceptive or capable chairperson?

USING AN OUTSIDER TO REVIEW
To make rapid progress in improving meetings across the whole organization it can be useful to use an outsider – anyone not familiar with your way of working – to act as 'coach'. Someone taking on this role would initially sit in the corner and observe the proceedings closely, if necessary making notes on what people say and do.

After the meeting is over, a process review can be conducted, with the participants, about how they perceived that particular meeting and how it could be improved. Confronting the meeting with questions rather than telling the participants what they have to do may prove fruitful. The role should be focused on helping the meeting to discover what they have to change to improve.

CONTINUING DEVELOPMENT OF MEETINGS

The involvement of an outsider should always be seen as helping the meeting process to help itself. As quickly as possible the coach should try to shift the responsibility for improvement back on to the in-house participants themselves.

As we have seen, one way of doing this is to encourage the chairperson to include a 'Review of the Meeting' in the agenda. Once this is working well, participants can be encouraged to consider ways in which the meeting could be improved for the future – not merely the current decisions and process, but in any way whatsoever.

Once the view has been concluded, it is important to decide on action to improve the conduct of the meeting. This crucial step is rarely taken. Too often meetings have analysed what is not working, and this knowledge is shared by every participant, yet nothing is done to change things.

Drawing out lessons or principles to guide future meetings, which are both practical and accepted by everyone, is the first important step forward. These new principles or procedures can then themselves be reviewed after a period of time, leading to new methods of working and an approach that can be termed 'continuous improvement' or 'learning to learn'.

Remember the old Chinese proverb:

A thousand mile journey begins with the first steps.

APPENDIX A
RULES OF ORDER

Everyone who chairs a formal meeting should be familiar with the basic concepts of *Roberts' Rules of Order*. In an ideal situation, where there is a good chairperson and effective contributions from participants, they should not be necessary. It is still advisable to know them, however, as there are certain circumstances where they can be extremely useful:

- For certain contentious items for short periods
- At the meetings of many civic and charitable organizations which are run along strict parliamentary lines

For detailed reference consult *Roberts' Rules of Order*, but the following are the key points of formal procedure:

(1) Any motion should be proposed and seconded before discussion of the issue starts. (This is to ensure that the subject deserves discussion.)
(2) The chairperson should restate the motion after it has been proposed so it is clear that it has been ruled in order. (This also helps the chairperson to control the meeting.)
(3) Only one main motion (one that brings an action before the group) can be considered at a time.
(4) A main motion can be changed or disposed of by a subsidiary motion. For example: 'I move that the minutes be amended to delete paragraph 5.' The subsidiary motion must be discussed and voted on before the main motion can be discussed and voted on, although it cannot be made unless the main motion is already under consideration, i.e. discussion of it has already begun.
(5) A privileged motion is one that calls for immediate

action of the whole meeting. For example, 'I move that we recess'. It must be considered before any other motion and is not debatable.

(6) A motion to reconsider a previous vote must be made by someone on the winning side.

(7) When someone 'calls for the previous question', it is only a suggestion to end the discussion and vote. If a single person objects, you must keep the discussion going. If someone 'moves the previous question' and there is a second, you must vote on whether or not to end the debate. If the motion fails, the discussion continues.

(8) As a general rule, do not attempt to draft any resolution that affects the constitution or conduct of the organization, longer than a single sentence, in a formal meeting. Refer it to a committee or back to staff.

APPENDIX B
MINUTES OF MEETINGS

The minutes of the meeting should be written by the meeting secretary as soon as possible, while the subjects are still fresh in the minds of both the secretary and the members. The minutes should be a brief but accurate account of the business transacted at the meeting.

In order to ensure an efficient business organization each meeting should be identifiable (by a reference number, for example) and a permanent record of the following items should be made.

- Where and when the meeting was held
- Who chaired the meeting
- Who was present
- Who sent their apologies, if absent
- A statement that the agenda was adhered to – e.g. that the minutes of the previous meeting were agreed and signed
- A few lines summarizing reports, including file numbers, so that members can obtain copies if they wish
- A summary of any discussion that followed the reports
- All motions and amendments in the exact form they were put by the chairperson
- The names of the proposer and seconder of each motion and amendment
- A summary of the main points of the discussion
- The number of those voting
- The decision taken on each proposal
- Who is taking what action and when
- The date of the next meeting

The secretary's task in writing the minutes of the meeting is to convey the flavour of the meeting and strength of opinion of the participants to those people who were unable to attend. People who did attend need to have confirmation of what they and their colleagues discussed and decided. This prevents subsequent arguments about what was actually agreed.

It is advisable to develop an impersonal style, avoiding dialogue or quoting from long-winded speeches. By doing this, you will ensure the facts are clear and not masked by unnecessary detail. Reduce long discussions to clear statements of the main points, which contain the essentials and avoid the 'waffle'.

Sometimes people adopt the procedure of agreeing the minutes at the meeting itself. In this case, the chairperson sums up the main arguments on either side of the discussion, states the decision reached and the participants' action, saying who does what and when. The secretary will then read back what the chairperson has dictated. Usually the group will assent without further discussion.

AFTER THE MEETING

A copy of the minutes should be sent to everybody who has a right or need to know as soon as possible. If writing the minutes is likely to be delayed, then some sort of interim action sheet should be sent.

The chairperson normally has the opportunity to check the minutes before they are sent out. In this way minor errors can be eliminated and misunderstandings avoided.

The writing of minutes can all too easily be seen as thankless drudgery but their role should not be overlooked. Accurate and timely minutes are essential to the overall progress and results of any regular meeting or committee.

APPENDIX C
HOW TO WRECK MEETINGS

It is interesting to look at the ways that meetings *can* be wrecked, so that those of you who wish to spot the tactic being used can take these methods into account. The following list is by no means exhaustive. So many of the words start with D that we decided to call it the eleven Ds to DEFEAT the meeting.

1. *Distract and disrupt.* Make a loud noise, talk about anything off the point, bring in subjects that are irrelevant, generally offer advice where it is not needed.
2. *Disagree.* Beg to differ, perhaps politely, but find ways of falling out with the main thrusts of everyone else's argument. Disagree on principle, disagree on fact, disagree with emotion.
3. *Defend and attack.* Related to number 2 is the use of defence and attack. Attack the people with whom you disagree and when they attack back defend even more vigorously. If you have the skill, introduce a hint of paranoia – that always seems to attract a decent crowd.
4. *Dominate.* Push your own points at the expense of others. If you have a powerful voice use it, if not wave your arms about, shuffle your papers, lean over and point at someone else's papers, but generally impose yourself on the meeting and ensure that no one else gets the same degree of time and space as you.
5. *Deviate.* Take things off the point and down alleyways that are of interest to you. Refer back to previous meetings when you did not get your way and say why you feel you should be recompensed. Tell people that this situation reminds you of that time back in '86 when you were Head of Public Relations for . . . and if your reminiscences don't work, try to

get someone else reminiscing – preferably the oldest and most sentimental participant at the meeting.

6. *Divide*. Ensure that you have spoken to each of the different lobby groups before the meeting and said different things to each one. Try to set one lobby against another and then sit back and watch the fun develop.

7. *Deride*. Generally imply that one or other member of the meeting is not quite telling the honest truth. Lines such as, 'but we all know what can be done with statistics like these,' or 'but have we heard what *really* caused the production manager to want to buy the Mark IV modification?', will cause enough of a stir. The waverers at the meeting will sense that there is too much smoke for there not to be a fire somewhere. With incompetent chairing they will probably not notice that it is you who is providing most of the smoke.

8. *Dubious data*. This is a particularly effective way of ruining a meeting with scientists and engineers. They tend to like data and factual arguments. So give them data and facts, but don't worry about whether any of them are accurate or not. Wave statistics, graphs and charts around with gay abandon. When challenged, imply that these are early provisional results and that a more detailed survey is being carried out. That should delay things by several months.

9. *Damn with faint praise*. Often used in conjunction with no 7. If someone uses the 'dubious data technique' on you then apply a serious and knowing eye to ripping the data apart. Say that the data they are quoting comes from material that was of use 10 years ago but things have changed now. Doubt the credibility of the people who collected the data, doubt the sanity of the people who added it up.

In looking for D's we found two other d-words that are

not well known but seem to apply very appropriately to certain kinds of wrecking techniques. The first is:

10. *Decrepitate,* which means to heat a substance until it admits a crackling sound. Otherwise known as baiting, or the corporate wind-up, this is when marketing gets back at personnel for all those appraisals, or production gets back at finance for all those forms, or just about anyone gets back at corporate planning. How many of us have been at meetings where decrepitation has occurred on a massive scale?

The other word that attracted our attention was:

11. *De-flocculate,* which means to disperse, forming a suspension. One of the best ways of wrecking a meeting is to reach no further conclusion and leave everything in suspense. De-flocculation is a favourite method of appearing to act but actually deciding nothing.

These descriptions of wrecking techniques are meant as a guide to what *not* to do. But even if your intentions are truly dishonourable, we hope that by exposing them, we have weakened their impact. None of these techniques will work in meetings that are well chaired and have competent and knowledgeable contributors.

Reproduced with kind permission from *Effective Meetings* by Philip and Jane Hodgson (Century Business 1992)

APPENDIX D
MEETINGS REVIEW: A GROUP TRAINING EXERCISE

(a) As an individual, decide whether you **AGREE** or **DISAGREE** with the following statements.

(b) As a group, reach a consensus decision on each item, rotating the chairperson's role after each statement.

AGREE/DISAGREE STATEMENTS   **RING**

1. Meetings are nearly always a waste of time   A   D

2. People attending a meeting should be encouraged to participate   A   D

3. Successful meetings depend upon a strong chairperson   A   D

4. The best number of members at a meeting is between five and seven   A   D

5. No concern need be felt about silent members on a committee, since their silence is invariably the result of agreement with what is being said   A   D

6. A meeting where all contributions are invited by and then addressed to the chairperson is usually efficient and productive   A   D

7. If meetings are to be held regularly, it is a good idea to rotate the chairperson's role among the members of the group   A   D

8. The chairperson's attitude to the meeting will be reflected in the attitudes of the group members to each other   A   D

9. When the chairperson is doing their best, one should not openly criticize or find fault with their conduct   A   D

10. Generally there comes a time when   A   D

democratic group methods must be abandoned in order to solve practical problems

11. It is sometimes necessary to ignore the feelings of others in order to reach a group decision   A   D

12. At decision-taking meetings too much emphasis is placed on whether the members are happy with the outcome, as opposed to whether the decision is the best one   A   D

13. There would be more attentiveness in meetings if the chairperson would get quickly to the point and say what they want the others to do   A   D

14. A meeting functions most efficiently when it ignores rather than discusses rivalries between members   A   D

15. The typical meeting would be improved if the chairperson imposed a firm discipline on the proceedings   A   D

REVIEW OF PARTICIPATION AT MEETINGS

The items listed below are some of the key aspects of running a more participative meeting. Rate meetings you have attended on each of the eight items by circling the appropriate number.

1. How much do participants feel they belong at the meeting?

1	2	3	4	5
Participants have no sense of belonging	Not close but some friendly relations	About average sense of belonging	Warm sense of belonging	Strong sense of belonging

2. How much do participants listen to each other?

1	2	3	4	5
No listening	Little listening	Average listening	Considerable listening	Remarkable listening

3. How much openness at the meeting?

1	2	3	4	5
No openness	Some openness	Average openness	Considerable openness	Remarkable openness

4. How much attention is paid to process?
(The procedure, interaction and feelings)

1	2	3	4	5
No attention	Little attention	Some attention	Fair amount	Much attention

5. How much attention is paid to the task?
(The technical or task work)

1	2	3	4	5
No attention	Little attention	Some attention	Fair amount	Much attention

6. How are decisions made?

1	2	3	4	5
Unable to reach decisions	Made by a few or by one person	By majority vote	Attempts at integrating minority vote	Full participation and tested consensus

7. How are leadership needs met?

1	2	3	4	5
Not met, drifting	Leadership concentrated in one person	Some leadership sharing	Leadership functions distributed	Leadership functions distributed very appropriately to the task *and* the people

8. How well are resources utilized?

1	2	3	4	5
One or two contributed	Several tried to contribute but were discouraged	Average use of group resources	Group resources well used and encouraged	Group resources fully and effectively used

REFERENCES

Bell, G. (1990) *The Secrets of Successful Business Publishing*, London: Heinemann Professional Publishing

A practical and down-to-earth book containing many useful checklists on how to run better business meetings

Hodgson, P. and J. (1992) *Effective Meetings*, London: Century Business.

A comprehensive book on every aspect of meetings, containing a blend of theory, checklists and practical examples

Johnson, R.A., Robinson, L., Jewett, M. *et al*. (1987) *How To Run Better Business Meetings*, Maidenhead: McGraw-Hill.

An excellent book on the use of visual aids (including computer graphics) at meetings, as well as useful guidance on planning and preparation.

Kiefer, G.D. (1988) *The Strategy of Meetings*, London: Piatkus.

A comprehensive examination of the ways of presenting yourself at meetings, and the underlying politics involved.

Laborde, G.Z. (1983) *Influencing With Integrity*, Palo Alto: Syntony Publishing.

A book about communications in general, and neuro-linguistic programming in particular, with an excellent section on how to improve meetings.

Rackham, N. and Morgan, P. (1977) *Behaviour Analysis in Training*, Maidenhead: McGraw-Hill.

A book about interactive skills in general which includes some first class research on the role of the chairperson as well as on how participants can contribute more effectively at meetings.

Also published by Century Business

HOW TO NEGOTIATE
YOUR SALARY
Tips, gambits and strategies for getting
the package you deserve

ALAN JONES

Everything you need to know to enter into salary discussions
confident of gaining the total remuneration package (TRP)
that you want and deserve.

Whether negotiating a salary for a new job or requesting a
pay rise in a current job, this is the ideal guide if you feel
that your negotiation skills could benefit from some fine-
tuning.

Complete with action checklists and practical examples, *How
to Negotiate Your Salary* is another readable and effective
book from the author of *How to Write a Winning CV* and
How to Build a Successful Career.

Alan Jones is a leading outplacement consultant and
freelance writer.

Paperback £7.99
208 pp   216 x 135 mm
0712653910

MAKING A COMEBACK

A woman's guide to returning to work
after a break

MARGARET KORVING

The message is clear – there has never been a better time for
women returning to work. A sharp decline in school-leavers
means that employers are turning to previously ignored
'minorities' – like working mothers and the young retired –
to meet the skills shortages that now threaten them.

But just how easy is it to step back on to the career ladder
after a long period spent bringing up your children or caring
for elderly relatives – a period in which technology has
changed the workplace out of all recognition? How do you
develop a career and keep your family content? What
provisions, in terms of child care and training opportunities,
are really being made by employers and government to
entice women back into full-time careers?

Making A Comeback examines in detail the recent changes in
prospects for women returners. It looks at what is on offer,
and gives down-to-earth advice on how to select, train for
and secure a new and exciting career – without neglecting
your home or family.

Margaret Korving is one of Britain's most popular and
experienced careers experts. She was careers consultant to
the *Daily Telegraph* for 18 years.

Paperback £5.99
136 pp   216 x 135 mm
0091744156

HOW TO READ THE FINANCIAL PAGES

A simple guide to the way money works and the jargon

MICHAEL BRETT

This is an expanded, third edition of the bestselling and definitive guide to the City of London, its markets and how they are written up in the financial pages. The book has been fully revised to include all the radical changes that have taken place in the City since Big Bang, and covers among other topics the interlocking and interacting worlds of the gilt-edged markets, the money market and the ERM.

Anyone who needs to understand the language of finance and the markets will find this book essential. A permanent fixture on Top Ten Business Bookseller lists, it strips away the jargon and mystique cloaking much of the City's activity and explains clearly how to 'read between the lines' of financial pages and reports.

Michael Brett, former editor of *Investors Chronicle,* is a financial journalist and lecturer at City University.

Paperback £8.99
312 pp   216 x 135 mm
0091748895

HOW TO BE HEADHUNTED

The art of building and sustaining your professional reputation

YVONNE SARCH

'Headhunting', or using the services of an executive search consultant, is now big business. Mergers, acquisitions and buyouts are commonplace, leading to a rapid turnover of top executives. In an increasing number of cases, such executives do not need to look for new organizations – the organizations find them.

But how do these sought-after high-flyers create such a flattering and rewarding demand for themselves? Are they simply the most able, hard-working and attractive people in their fields, or do they consciously adopt a detailed strategy for making themselves visible; for getting themselves and their achievements noticed by the 'right' people?

Written by one of Britain's top executive consultants (who was herself headhunted for her present top position), *How to be Headhunted* is a frank and authoritative guide to developing your professional profile and your career – both inside and outside the office. Aimed specifically at those who already have the qualifications, experience and ambition necessary for the jobs they want, it shows how to develop the self-worth, charisma and reputation demanded by professional recruiters.

Yvonne Sarch is a director of SSI, a major executive search firm.

Paperback £7.99
240 pp   234 x 153 mm
0712698957

GETTING TO YES

Negotiating agreement without giving in

ROGER FISHER & WILLIAM URY

A completely revised, second edition of the book recognized worldwide as the most effective guide to the negotiation game.

Successful negotiation is a core component of individual achievement. *Getting to Yes* provides practical strategies for getting what you want while keeping your adversaries happy. Its powerful, easily mastered principles will see you through no matter what the other side resorts to!

This edition includes a new introduction and many new examples, as well as the authors' answers to the ten most commonly asked questions about *Getting to Yes*.

A vitally important book for anyone dealing with other people in business, politics, diplomacy or counselling.

Roger Fisher is Williston Professor of Law at Harvard Law School and Director of the Harvard Negotiation Project.
William Ury is a specialist in negotiation and Associate Director of the Harvard Negotiation Project.

Paperback £5.99
176 pp   198 x 126 mm
071265528X

GETTING PAST NO

Negotiating with difficult people

WILLIAM URY

A sequel to all-time bestseller *Getting to Yes,* this new book
from international negotiation guru William Ury tackles the
very thorniest aspect of the subject: dealing with people who
won't deal.

What if the other side doesn't *want* to get to yes?

What if their answer is no? How do you negotiate with such
difficult people?

William Ury has simplified and distilled the techniques of
negotiation with unwilling adversaries into five basic and
universal principles, illustrated with a host of examples and
techniques on which to draw in difficult situations. Whether
your opponents are obstructive, offensive or downright
deceptive, *Getting Past No* provides success strategies for
everyone who has to negotiate: businesspeople, lawyers,
politicians, diplomats and trade union leaders.

William Ury is an internationally recognized expert on
negotiation and Associate Director of the Harvard
Negotiation Project.

Paperback £5.99
164 pp   198 x 126 mm
0712655239